TRANSFORMING:

The Power of Leading
from Identity

TRANSFORMING

The Power of Leading
from Identity

GREG WALLACE

Published by The Wallace Group, LLC
981 West Arrow Highway, Suite 322 San
Dimas, California, USA 91773
www.thewallacegroup.org

ISBN 13 -- 978-0-9964493-3-5

ISBN 10 -- 0-9964493-3-7

Edited by Donna Scuderi
Cover Design by Gus Jimenez

Contents

Prologue

Leadership is a buzzword backed by a $24.5 billion industry.[1] You know where the money is being spent. Seminars, workshops, books, and digital media are cranked out by great leaders and snapped up by those who want to be. No doubt, the industry is doing some people some good some of the time. But as robust as the market is, and with massive volumes of material being consumed, you would think brilliant leadership would be evident *everywhere*.

There are great leaders—lots of them. But there is also a very real leadership deficit plaguing all sectors of society. Why is it that millions earnestly strive for greatness, but never quite catch the wave? They have attended the seminars and devoured the books. They have tried the formulas and emulated the best of the best, only to come up short of the greatness they desire.

In her book, *The End of Leadership*, Barbara Kellerman laments, "The tireless teaching of leadership has brought us no closer to leadership nirvana than we were previously."[2] Ms. Kellerman is the James MacGregor Burns Lecturer in Public Leadership at Harvard University's John F. Kennedy School of Government, which makes her conclusion all the more sobering.

Having been immersed in leadership literature and its application throughout my professional life, I believe the problem is not that billions are spent on leadership training, but that leadership training is too often based on flawed premises. We have

1

been mistaken about *how* one becomes a great leader. We have invested so heavily in the traits and methods of others that we have overlooked the unique qualities of the individual and forgotten that each leader's personal identity is the real stuff of leadership.

Therefore, I concur with Ms. Kellerman's assertion that the problem is at least partly due to "mistaken assumptions,"[3] including the belief that "leadership is static," that "leadership can be taught," that it "can be learned quickly and easily," and that "one form of leadership can be taught, simultaneously, to different people in different situations."[4]

Despite the lack of definitive data, we can reasonably conclude that much of the billions of dollars spent on leadership development each year involves the attempt to teach the same leadership model, at the same time, to different people working in different situations. I won't presume to call these approaches ineffective. They do, however, seem incomplete.

Writing the complete leadership book is not my mission. My reason for adding to the literature heap is to invite you to build your leadership story from the bricks and mortar of who you are, because I believe *the best way for unique individuals to become better leaders is to develop unique leadership models rooted in their individual identities.*

Some of the best guidance I have found on developing individual leadership models did not come from leadership "gurus" (many of whom I regard very highly, by the way) but from the Indiana High

School Athletic Association's handbook for team leaders, which offers this sage advice:

"We feel it is important to emphasize that no one right way exists to be an effective, dynamic captain.... The ultimate goal of this book is that you use it as a reference or guide in constructing your own Captain's Handbook. Feel free to develop your own notes and definition that apply to you, your coaches, and your team. Add your own ideas and perspectives, and then pass it down to future captains. This way, you can leave your own legacy."[5]

My goal in writing *this book* is precisely that you would use it as a guide in constructing your own leadership principles. To that end, I share the details of a leadership assignment I was privileged to undertake—not just the high points, but the messy moments in the trenches. My hope is that my story will help bring yours into focus, not by offering a compelling list of "shoulds," but by creating space for your unique leadership principles to emerge.

So, go ahead and jot down the ideas that reflect your point of view. Let them spring organically from the person you are and the leader you are continually becoming. Then pass them down to future leaders, not as a set of legalisms, but as evidence that each and every leader's story is unique.

Let that be *your* legacy.

Leading from
Identity

Introduction

I once heard a lobbyist say about a politician, "He wants to *be* governor, but he does not want to *do* governor." And, yes, it was meant to be dismissive.

The lobbyist's audience, primarily leaders, laughed. That's because leaders are trained to *do* leadership, and to be the best possible doers of leadership by focusing on skills development. So when the guy in the governor's mansion is derided for wanting to *be* but not *do*, where is the disconnect? Leadership expert, Dr. Barbara Kellerman notes:

"Notwithstanding the enormous sums of money and time that have been poured into trying to teach people how to lead, over its roughly forty-year history the leadership industry has not in any major, meaningful, measurable way improved the human condition."[6]

The indictment is stunning! I propose that the issue is one of focus. It's time to shift from *doing* leadership to *being* leaders, and from trying to learn a single form of leadership to leading from our individual, unique identities. This type of leading focuses more on *being* than on *doing*, and it is influenced more by identity than by skill sets. Here's why identity is so important: when we come under pressure or are thrust into unfamiliar and uncomfortable situations, *who we are* affects our actions more than *what we are taught*. I have found that, because we are not practiced at emphasizing the best of who we are, our best side does not always shine in pressurized situations.

Some years ago I was invited into a pressurized situation: I was hired to manage an organization's operations and to participate in changing its culture. I jumped in head first. Before the effective date of my hire, I had several conversations with the owner about how I would undertake my assignment. I also designed and gained approval for a needs assessment. It was a nine-page, single-spaced beauty. I even created a corresponding presentation for the owner, complete with talking points to help him launch the quest. Call it intuition, common sense, or the hand of God, but I soon realized that I might be pushing too hard, too fast. I shelved the needs assessment and decided to focus on *being* rather than *doing*. Instead of emphasizing the organization's vision, goals, and strategy, I focused on being trustworthy, caring, and unselfish.

My first presentation to the management team was not solely about work; it was about helping them know me better. Thus began a relationship based on trusting who I was rather than what I could do. Trust brought the credibility to suggest change initiatives without creating enemies. As Woodrow Wilson famously said, "If you want to make enemies, try to change something." I discovered that I could make changes and build relationships, too.

This and other leadership assignments showed that simply being who I am allowed me to become a better leader and more effective contributor in developing high-performing organizations.

This idea flies in the face of conventional wisdom. Legion are the books that recommend shelving aspects of one's identity in order to embrace the "right" traits of successful leadership.

Examples are everywhere. In offering popular leadership books, booksellers promote the idea that most leaders are not born leaders. They suggest that anyone with sufficient passion to succeed could learn a set of principles and become a great leader. Countless books trumpet particular leadership models; countless more enshrine the examples of particular leaders. Consider this review of a book about General Colin Powell's success: "Powell appears to be a natural born leader with an intuitive sense of strategy for advancement in war and politics. For those of us who are not so lucky to have such diplomacy inherently, [the author's] book can teach us how to lead effectively following Powell's example."[7]

The book is informative, and much can be learned from studying great leaders. Yet, I agree with Dr. Kellerman: the efficacy of cultivating certain leadership traits or imitating favorite role models, at least as primary drivers of leadership development, is questionable. The pursuit of "tried and true" models keeps some of us reading piles of books that we hope will bridge the gap between how we see ourselves and how we see ourselves as leaders.[8] But is the gap the real issue?

Popular culture heralds the notion that the best natural leaders are extroverts. Many consultants and authors buy into the idea, to the dismay of introverts everywhere. The following comments from an introvert reading a particular leadership book should come as no surprise:

"The author is clearly an extrovert so some of the personality traits he talks about or things he sort of assumes you are already doing are only valid if you are also extroverted like him. For those of us who are introverts, you are going to realize that there are extra steps involved to reach some of his suggested goals/mindsets...."[9]

Unfortunately, the popularized version of leadership tempts some of us introverts to park on the leadership sidelines. We tell ourselves that we could never be good leaders because we are not charismatic enough. *But we are wrong.* In my (mostly) humble opinion, each of us is capable of influencing people to good outcomes (which is my definition of good leadership). We needn't acquire a particular set of traits or emulate other people's personalities to succeed. Good leadership starts with our own identities, and with knowing and remaining true to who we are. It is not about trying to be someone else or squeezing ourselves into other people's molds. It is about being one mold among many, and allowing ourselves to be the unique people and leaders we were created to be.

1

Identity

Leadership starts with *identity*.[10] You have your identity and I have mine. That is as it should be. So why would any one leadership model work for both of us? It wouldn't. The best leadership model either of us can follow is the one we develop for ourselves—the one that demonstrates the organic inseparability of leadership style from personal identity.

Karp and Helgø make the leadership-identity connection saying, "Leadership is perhaps better understood as identity construction."[11] Because leaders act, the researchers also say that "leadership is therefore action," and "such action is made possible by the way leaders construct their identities as leaders."[12] In other words, how we lead is based on how we perceive our identities. Karp and Helgø conclude that leadership identity is more important than skills, characteristics, or traits.[13] I second their conclusion and the liberating emotions that go with it.

This book provides a truthful example[14] of what happens when we use our life experiences (how we were raised; the influences of relatives, coaches, mentors, and bosses; the lessons we learn from The School of Hard Knocks; the nuggets of wisdom we glean from seminars and books, etc.) to develop our own leadership principles. However, my goal is not to offer yet another set of principles to follow. My hope is that each of us leads more effectively, not from someone else's identity but from our own (even the introverts among us).

Before I share how I used my principles to help my group reach their personal and workplace goals, allow me to share a couple of caveats (or perhaps they are admissions):

First, I recognize that certain "tried and true" leadership principles warrant consideration regardless of our uniqueness as leaders. For example, leaders everywhere pledge allegiance to the principle (however variously worded and practiced) that says, "Build people; don't use them."

Second, I acknowledge that *being* ultimately leads to *doing*. Here's why *being* is so important: the quality of our being affects the quality of our doing. Peter Drucker has been quoted as saying that "leadership is defined by results not attributes."[15] Principles are critically important, not in and of themselves, but because they steer leaders to make good choices that lead to effective actions that produce good results.

Finally, I acknowledge that *principle* is defined in various ways. One dictionary defines it as "a basic belief, theory, or rule that has a major *influence* on the way in which something is done...a basic rule or belief about what is right and morally good, that *influences* the way that you behave and the way that you treat other people...."[16] In the context of this book, *a principle is a guidepost that influences the way we behave and/or the way we treat other people.*

Whatever we call the principles developed in this book— whether *laws*, *rules*, or *truths*—I would suggest that, as leaders, it is important to develop sound guideposts for our behavior and interaction with others. Few would deny that how we behave and how we treat others are key drivers in determining the quality of our results.

Bearing all this in mind, what follows is an account of how following the principles I claim as my own led me to produce excellent results. I believe that if you develop, adopt, and follow your own principles, you can create great results, too.

I believe the chapters ahead will help you to do just that.

Leading a Turnaround

2

The Opportunity

It was one of those "I remember where I was" moments. The memory is vivid, in part because the moment was an answer to prayer. The anxiety I felt afterward is another good reason it sticks in my mind.

"It" was a phone call from my boss in April of 2009. Ed Wesley was Vice President of the Customer-Facing Operations Department (CFO) in the Customer Contact Business Unit of a large financial services company, Towncenter Consumer Services (TCS).

I had been at TCS for eighteen years. For all but nine months of that time I'd held staff roles as an attorney, in various human resources functions including labor, staffing, equal opportunity, and training. I had also served in procurement and planning. For nearly six years, I worked in CFO, where Ed hired me to implement my own advice— advice I gave when I was still CFO's HR account manager and the director in charge of HR for the business unit. (My direct reports were the account managers for the unit's other departments; CFO was by far the unit's largest department.)

After Ed was hired, I led an organizational assessment of CFO, which was just a few years old. The department was a consolidation of five major operational groups, all of which were led by directors with more than fifteen years' experience. For years those groups had reported directly to the business unit's leader, a senior vice president.

Although the organizations were consolidated under a single umbrella, the separate visions, missions, values, and business plans developed within each remained in place. Not surprisingly, one major recommendation from the assessment was the development of an organization-wide infrastructure. The unit needed an overarching strategy, a single budget, shared support functions, and an organization- wide culture rooted in a team orientation of vision, mission, and values. In other words, five organizations needed to become one.

My recommendations, my responsibility—that's the way Ed saw it. So he asked me to build and lead a new group named Strategy and Support. The assignment was intense because it meant changing the organization's culture. It was also extremely satisfying, because I was helping to bring my own recommendations to life.

When it launched, Strategy and Support contained six separate functions: business processes and technology, benchmarking, communications, training, organizational change, and planning. It also included an unnamed chief-of- staff function. Over the next five years or so, three of the six distinct functions and significant parts of two others were consolidated into other business units or corporate organizations. At the time of Ed's 2009 phone call, my scope of responsibilities had dwindled to such an extent that I was praying about whether it was time to move on. I was a director but my scope of responsibilities had narrowed. I was leading the training function, supporting CFO's alignment with the business unit's planning activities, and acting as Ed's *de facto* chief of staff.

The phone call quite literally answered my prayer. Because it presented an opportunity I had been more or less been ducking for over a decade, it also raised my anxiety level. More than one mentor or other leader had already encouraged me "to get some hair on my chest" and "see what it's like in the real world" by "getting out into the field" and working in an operational organization.

Acknowledging the validity of their counsel, I always nodded my head (but not too enthusiastically) when asked if I'd be willing to take an assignment in an operations group. Secretly I wondered whether I could make the switch.

What a wimp!

That April phone call laid the challenge at my feet. I could lead an operations group, not just as a developmental opportunity, but as a real "You are accountable for producing results, son" assignment. It was not in the field, exactly, but in an office environment. Apparently, even God knew I was a wimp.

Nevertheless, it was an opportunity to put my money where my mouth was, and to practice what I had been preaching about how to lead and manage people and improve an organization.

Although I was a little anxious, I looked forward to it.

3

The Work Group

The Application and Payment Processing Division (APP) was less than two years old. About six months earlier it had been transferred from the Credit Services and Programs Organization (CS&P) to CFO, to be joined with CFO's other operational groups. After the transfer, CS&P's division leaders went from being colleagues of APP leaders to being their clients.

The weeks and months following the transition had not gone smoothly. For one thing APP was led by a senior manager, whereas each of CS&P's divisions was led by a director. In the company's hierarchical culture, this put APP at a disadvantage. The opportunity to lead APP opened up when its senior manager accepted a position in another business unit and I was asked to take her place. CS&P was accustomed to treating APP like the new kid on the block, specifically *their* new kid. Given the organizational history, CS&P did not view the senior manager as a peer, but as a matrixed direct report. The senior manager's direct reports, Roman Anderson and Rachel Williams, had not been in middle management very long. They knew their work but were getting a crash course in influence, as in "how to influence people without having positional authority."

Anecdotal evidence suggested that CS&P management and APP did not see eye to eye on the level of service the latter was providing the former. I would soon confirm that evidence in face-to-face meetings with CS&P officers, directors, and managers. A few weeks later, when one of the CS&P directors introduced me to his new boss (the Vice President of CS&P), he did so by declaring, "If anyone can turn around APP, Greg can." It was a great endorsement for me, but not so much for APP.

Thus, I was welcomed to my first opportunity to lead an operations group. My initial anxiety aside, I was enthusiastic about my assignment. TCS was a good company known for being a good corporate citizen, and I was now positioned to contribute to the well-being of its customers and internal organizations. TCS prided itself on being consumer-friendly. Through CS&P, the company offered a wide variety of financial services, and although its name did not reflect it, the company was branching out by adding small commercial clients. The Application and Payment Processing group supported CS&P programs both for individual and commercial consumers. Besides APP's data entry of all applications, the group also handled end-to-end management of the process, including business processing and information technology support.

TCS used various marketing activities to increase its business. It regularly operated rebate programs, promoted annual percentage-rate reductions, and offered other incentives. In addition to processing millions of dollars annually from rebates and other incentives, APP also processed the enrollment applications for those programs.

APP played a critical role, its formation being based on the promise that a centralized processing function for TCS' highest-volume programs would decrease costs and improve efficiency. APP was struggling to fulfill that promise. As Albert Einstein is credited with saying, "In the middle of difficulty lies opportunity."[17]

I was about to find out whether that was true.

4

The Challenges

It didn't take me long to identify APP's most significant challenges. At the top of the list was its struggle to transition from being a start-up to an ongoing operation. For the sake of its employees and the benefit of its clients, an organizational identity had to be created, as no consensus existed regarding APP's primary roles and responsibilities.

As already mentioned, APP's leader was a senior manager tasked (unenviably) with asking directors in another organization to change their way of working. The senior manager was supported by Roman and Rachel, the fledgling middle managers also mentioned earlier. Though skilled subject-matter experts, they were taking huge steps up from their previous level of responsibility. The dynamics were fraught with difficulty, the difference in positional authority between CS&P's directors and APP's senior manager being only part of the problem. CS&P program managers, who were used to seeing APP's middle managers and client relationship managers as "subordinates," were now being asked to view them as peers.

Roman and Rachel responded by trying to please the CS&P program managers through attentive customer service. For example, most programs were well staffed to minimize delays in program restarts and to ensure quick, accurate processing of applications. For this, the two middle managers came under intense criticism (more on that later).

Another key challenge for APP were the ebbs and flows in demand. Periods of scant activity were followed by surges of high volume. The changes happened over relatively short periods of time. Because of the volatility, approximately 60 percent of APP's frontline work force was supplemental. These workers were officially the employees of TenPenny Workforce Solutions (TWS), TCS's vendor for such services. When volume was low, supplemental workers were released; when volume was high they were brought on board.

Credit card program managers in CS&P were keenly interested in the size of this supplemental workforce, because APP's labor costs hit their budgets. They were also attentive to the metrics regarding turnaround time. If APP retained a relatively large work force to ensure swift processing of applications, the budget increased. If they kept labor costs too tightly reined, application processing slowed down. Because of this interplay, APP also had client relationship managers serving as liaisons with CS&P's credit card program managers. The two groups worked to strike a balance between costs and productivity, while protecting their mutual interests in the quality of the work being performed.

To say that when I arrived CS&P program managers had not fully transitioned to seeing APP as a peer organization would be an enormous understatement. To say that when I left three years later the program managers were willing partners of APP gives me a great deal of satisfaction.

5

Overcoming (Spoiler Alert!)

In April of 2009 I assumed leadership of APP. In January of 2010 we officially launched a project called the Value Proposition Initiative (VPI). Among its primary goals were (1) to establish APP's value proposition, and (2) to work with CS&P to delineate APP's role and responsibilities. The goals were met. Based on the publicly declared value proposition and its agreed upon roles and responsibilities, APP's leadership team established 2010 goals and initiatives.

In March of 2011, APP reported its 2010 results. To enhance the stats' credibility and acceptance, we asked an internal auditor to review the methodology for how the stats were compiled as well as the accuracy of the stats. Among the encouraging results were:

- a 4.6 percent increase in the number of applications APP processed;

- a 36 percent reduction in the average cost per application;

- a 32 percent decrease in the error-rate percentage for commercial programs; and

- a 15 percent jump in productivity.

By the end of 2011, APP had generated so much confidence in its efficient, high-quality, cost-effective processing of applications that CS&P senior managers transferred or were in the process of transferring the processing function for several of their lower-volume, more specialized programs to APP. In addition, APP middle managers and client relationship managers were taking thought leadership roles in further consolidating the processing function under a central umbrella.

How did this turnaround happen? Although concepts such as "robust dialogue"[18] (from Larry Bossidy and Ram Charan) and "begin with the end in mind" [19] (from Stephen R. Covey) influenced me, I relied upon principles I developed or adopted in three primary areas: leadership, people, and organization. In Chapter 6 I will summarize those principles and their development.

Now that you have the backstory and a brief overview on APP, the coming chapters will reveal exactly how those principles contributed to the division's stunning turnaround. My hope is that you will be inspired to develop your own principles, that you will become more intentional about self- development, and that you will discover the joys and benefits of leading out of your own identity.

Putting the Principles to Work

6

The Principles

From a leadership perspective, how did APP, an organization whose clients wanted to strip away some of its work, become an organization whose clients wanted to entrust it with more responsibility? How did I lead this turnaround, and how was it possible to do it almost exclusively with the same leadership team?

Here's a hint: I did not rely upon highly-touted leadership traits, even when they were touted by leaders I highly respected. I did not follow a particular leadership model or a particular leadership role model. I was just *me*—a me who was intentional about putting into practice all that I had learned and become. Certain principles had been instilled in me; some were "borrowed" from others. I lived all of them and learned some in The School of Hard Knocks. In other words, I relied on my own identity—the sum total of "me"—more than on any particular set of skills, characteristics, or traits.

What follows is a summary of my principles and how I developed them. There are areas of overlap, as you will see, but I have divided the principles into three categories: leadership, people, and organization.

Leadership Principles: Don't Just Do. Be!

Too often leaders get caught up in doing "stuff" to get results; but by also *being*—leading out of my identity—I was able to change APP's culture and set the stage for organizational success. The following are five leadership principles upon which I relied:

1. Be Trustworthy

People follow only leaders they trust; they trust only leaders they know. To become known, leaders must establish relationship.

A fellow student in a leadership training seminar germinated this aspect of my understanding on trust. The slightly catchy description of the concept comes largely from what he said. The idea is this: trust is important and trust comes from relationship. My fellow student was Norm, an executive vice president from one of the major television networks. Wherever you are, Norm, thanks! And thanks to my wife, Linda, who helped me to understand that *everything* begins with relationship.

2. Be First

Model the behavior you expect.

This principle came straight from my upbringing: Don't ask anyone to do anything you are unwilling to do. This was a particular emphasis from my dad, a former Army staff sergeant who served in Vietnam. He was not a "do as I say, not as I do" type of parent. He thought it was important that my brother and I be respectful, be on time, and keep our word. So he was respectful, he arrived on time, and he kept his word. I also remember my dad doing his homework. He received his associate of arts degree at the local community college on the same day I graduated from elementary school. Dad was a living example, and his example stuck.

3. Be There for the People

Serve the people. Real leadership is servant-leadership.

This is another "oldie but goodie" from my parents. It is easy to understand, but doesn't happen all by itself. It demands intentionality. I remember being seventeen and telling my mom how excited a sales associate was to receive a compliment from me during an extremely busy time at a tux shop. My mom seemed pretty excited about it, too. "That's something your dad would have done," she said. That's a compliment I'll never forget. Servant-leadership is a rewarding proposition for everyone.

4. Be An Enabler
(Empower People to Do Good Work)

Do not micromanage.

One of my former bosses modeled the idea of letting good people do what they do best. As my boss and mentor, she taught me a lot and gave me the room to put into practice what I had learned. As a result, I learned even more about the work and about myself. In essence, she allowed my identity to unfold as she maximized my capabilities.

5. Be Good

More than doing well, we also want to do good.

My mom and dad would be proud that I am doing my best to live out another of their teachings. Although they loved it when my brother and I brought home report cards filled with *A's* and *B's*, they also scanned the *E's* (for "excellent"), *S's* (for satisfactory), and *U's* (for unsatisfactory). They were looking for marks that reflected solid work habits and cooperation. They told my brother and me that they would be OK with a low grade in a subject *if* we received *E's* in work habits and cooperation. That standard was put to the test when I came home with a *D* in Spanish, but *E's* in work habits and cooperation. My parents passed the test, and in doing so, reinforced the importance of doing good over doing well.

People Principles:
It's All about the People

As my training manager constantly reminded me, "It's about the people." From her I learned the importance of getting out of my office and interacting with folks. I didn't do it "for show." Anything that is about people is about relationships. Within the context of relationship, these principles helped motivate people to give their best.

6. Involve the People

People support only the change they help to create.

This principle is not an original, but it's powerfully wise, so I adopted it.[20] In one of my HR roles, an internal client once told me "Don't do HR *to* me. Do HR *for* me." In other words, "Don't bring me your solution and then force me to use it, especially if doesn't work. Just work with me to craft a solution that will actually help me."

Point taken. It is easy to spout ideas based on best practices, without considering whether they are best for the unique organizations and people we serve. This principle reminds me to involve the people who know what they need. When I do, they feel supported and they become *supportive*.

7. Celebrate the People

We all want to be where we are celebrated, not where we are tolerated.

Celebrating people is a privilege. My wife, Linda, a tremendous leader in her own right, was instrumental in teaching me this principle. She and I both know people who have left their jobs because they felt tolerated. We have also watched people blossom where they were celebrated. Recognizing people for their excellence is a win-win: it affirms them and produces more of the excellence that benefits all parties.

8. Be among the People

People follow only leaders they trust; they trust only leaders they know. Trust comes out of relationship. (Yes, you have heard this before.)

My friend and colleague, Shelly Mercer, gets credit for this principle. Shelly is a wonderful example of producing great results by leading out of identity. Being among the people was a big part of her success, and my transformation. If not for her, I might still be managing from behind a desk, as though leading were a theory in a manual. Until I became more people-oriented, and therefore more knowable, she reminded me often: "It's all about the people." Translation: "Don't live behind your desk. You are not a solo act." Message received.

9. Create Work/Life Balance for the People...Even at Work

We work to live; we don't live to work. It's OK to be intentional about having fun at work. Ice-Cream Float Fridays, anyone?

If work is the only thing that gets your juices flowing, you are probably selling that model to your organization. But don't worry, there's a principle for that, compliments of Shelly and her leadership team. They made a special effort to bring the right balance to the work environment. They cared intensely about their profession, so they worked hard. But because they also cared for people, they played hard with their colleagues. It made for a healthier, more inspired, and more welcoming environment. A little balance goes a long way.

10. Empower the People to Do Good

Empowering people to do well is important; encouraging them to do good is important, too.

When you exemplify doing good, you effectively establish the expectation that your team members will treat one another with love, honor, and respect. By visibly rewarding appropriate behaviors, you reinforce your expectations and empower your team to deliver.

Earlier, I explained how my parents valued my doing the right thing. Once, when I was tempted to renege on a commitment to help someone with a Saturday project (so I could, uh, go with friends to an amusement park), I learned an important lesson about how to inspire good works in others. Instead of instructing me to keep my commitment, my dad asked me a series of questions about what integrity looked like. Then he gave me the space to make my own decision. Years later, the lesson is still bearing fruit: I not only strive to do right; I empower my team to do right.

Organizational Principles: Leveraging Purpose

To achieve culture change and empower high-performing, highly-motivated people to support it, both must be supported by organizational infrastructure. In changing the culture of APP, the following organizational principles leveraged the other changes made and supported by the people.

11. Begin with the Purpose in Mind
Ask: What does success look like?

If you don't know where you are going, any road will get you there. That might sound like yesterday's cliché; it is true nonetheless. Without a picture of your desired outcomes in mind, you are strapped on a rocket to nowhere. Stephen Covey's "begin with the end in mind"[21] had something to do my incorporating this principle. So did my training as a facilitator. One of the "tools" I learned to use was a simple question posed to a group engaged in a planning process: "What does success look like?" With their desired end result in mind, the group was able to formulate the right steps to achieve it.

12. Be Purposeful, but Patient
Be quick; but don't be in a hurry.

This principle is a classic I learned from one of my bosses (who may or may not have gotten it from the coaching great, John Wooden.)[22]   Time after time, I   watched   my boss patiently wait for all the ducks to line up in a row before he launched a project, even if the building was burning down around him. When he was eager to create a new and improved Customer-Facing Operations Department, he patiently waited for months until I was available to lead his Strategy and Support group. The School of Hard Knocks has confirmed the soundness of his approach many times: whenever I have responded to a problem prematurely (because I couldn't stand the dysfunction any longer), the problem took longer to solve.

13. Clarify Purpose
Clearly state the purpose, and garner the buy-in you need to succeed.

The School of Hard Knocks also drilled this principle into my being. Although getting buy-in from others is a time- consuming process of communicating purpose and value, the time is wisely spent. Hindsight reveals that I reach my destination sooner when I invest in the buy-in, and I get there later (and worse for the wear and tear) when I rush ahead without it. The bottom line is simple: no buy-in means you are going the distance alone. If no one is following, you are not leading. (Ouch.)

14. Focus on Purpose

If you chase two rabbits, both will escape.

Double-mindedness means double the effort and none of the results. If you have been there, you know exactly what I mean. This concept deeply penetrated my thinking when I read *Built to Last*.[23] The idea is simple enough, and it works when you work it: clarify your purpose and resist everything that is nonessential to it. Divided vision will always drive you sideways. Keep your sights set on a specific outcome and on the unchanging core values that support your stated purpose. A single-minded sense of purpose can transform an organization's outcomes.

15. Align Everything with Purpose

Be sure your people, resources, performance metrics, etc. are compatible with your goals.

It is entirely possible to inadvertently sabotage your mission. Suppose, for example, that you are creating buy-in for team goals, but your compensation structure rewards individual achievement. The disconnect might be buried under layers of bureaucracy and tradition, but the fallout will happen in the open. Organizationally speaking, you are at cross-purposes with what you intend to achieve.

Personal experience and Labovitz and Rosansky's *The Power of*

Alignment[24] taught me the value of this principle. I learned that the obstacles to an organization's goals can be subtle in a deadly sort of way. Conversely, you can grease the wheels of success with some fairly inconspicuous tweaks. Simply put, alignment is golden.

These, in a nutshell, are the fifteen principles that helped me lead an organization to the fulfillment of its greatest expectations. Here's how it happened.

7

The Project

The fifteen principles just shared rarely roll out in order. Instead, they play out as the team journey unfolds. My APP assignment reveals the organic process as it occurs in real life. I am not proposing an ideology or set of tenets; I am offering examples that can illuminate some of your challenges. As you read, look for parallels and perspectives that apply to your current endeavor or inspire fresh principles that are wholly yours.

> ## *Be Trustworthy*
> *People follow only leaders they trust; they trust only leaders they know. To become known, leaders must establish relationship.*

One of my first goals when I assumed leadership of APP was to establish a relationship with my leadership team. So I scheduled a meeting. Most leaders (appropriately) focus on getting to know their individual team members but provide fewer opportunities to be known themselves. Therefore, even if leaders are trustworthy, those who don't know them will have a hard time finding it out. I wanted this meeting to make it easier.

Dialogue helps to break the ice, so I invite it. It's relaxed and cordial, but substantive. I ask questions such as "Do your team members know your favorite *anything* (sport, food, movie, television show, app)? Do they have any idea who you are as a person first?" The conversation helps us to get to know each other, but also shows where the organization's culture is headed.

I also strive to reveal my management style from the outset. So in the case of APP, I invited project managers, client relationship managers, supervisors, and the two middle managers to a meeting. Right off the bat, everyone knew that my management style was inclusive. At the same time, I hoped to convey that I don't take myself too seriously and that I appreciate humor in the work environment. So after sharing a little about myself, I said, "Enough about me, what about you? What do you think about me?" (You have to have a sense of humor to ask *that* question of people you are just getting to know!)

My purpose was to generate trust and empower managers through the free flow of information. For instance,

I shared what was shareable from my meetings with CS&P executives, including the high points of a meeting involving the business unit's executives. My intent was to create a complete feedback loop that would launch a journey of trust.

My next major meetings were with the leaders of APP's client organization, CS&P. I spoke to its vice president and four of its directors. There was definitely a lack of clarity, or at the very least, a lack of agreement about APP's role. More importantly, APP's clients questioned the value APP was providing. That is where the Value Proposition Initiative (VPI) came in. I proposed the project to my boss, and he agreed.

Involve the People
People support only the change they help to create.

By the end of June, I had outlined a preliminary scope of work. That's where another key principle kicked in. The purpose of the VPI was straightforward: "To gain clarity, both inside and outside of the organization, about the work performed by the APP group and the value of this work to the company." The benefits of the project could be summarized in one word: *clarity*.

Once I secured Ed's blessings, I wanted to involve key stakeholders. I brought in Roman and Rachel, APP's middle managers, to help develop the project's scope and to enlist their support for whomever would be managing it. I wanted the clients involved, too. The most critical part of the initiative was getting their feedback regarding APP and the people who worked there. Their responses to the most pressing questions—*What is APP's role? What are its responsibilities? What constitutes superior value?*—would determine how APP approached its work for the foreseeable future.

Having stakeholders involved gave all parties some team-building "skin in the game." It was a good start, but timing issues became unexpectedly complicated. With progress underway, the last thing I wanted were delays. I was tempted to do whatever was necessary to avoid them. But a crash landing is far worse than a stall. Hurrying was *not* the answer.

Be Purposeful, but Patient
Be quick; but don't be in a hurry.

Before we could start in earnest, I needed someone to run the project, preferably someone from outside the organization. There were hurdles to clear. First, I had to secure Human Resources' permission to add an APP position. The process was formidable and took several weeks to complete. Then Nancy, the candidate we selected, took ill. By the time she arrived, it was September.

Client discontent reigned during the unexpected two- month delay. I was sorely tempted to stem the negative tide by launching the project without Nancy. But I had learned the hard way (and from watching my boss) that half-baked beginnings for the sake of short-term relief were just that— half-baked.

Yes. A good plan well executed is better than a perfect plan never realized. But heaping additional responsibilities on an already overwhelmed management team would have been like tossing an anchor to someone who was drowning. I also knew that if I started a project with biased people, I would forfeit the benefit of hearing the objective observations, responses, and actions only a neutral party like Nancy could provide.

It was worth waiting for someone without ties to APP or its client organization. So I waited. When Nancy arrived, I was more than ready to throw her into the deep end of the pool with a robust "Go forth and VPI!" There was just one hitch. Nancy knew nothing and no one from APP.

It was perfectly clear that the project would benefit from Nancy's getting to know the people and involving them in her rollout process. But the waiting game was wearing thin. (Insert "deep sigh" here.) I and the team were purposeful, but out of patience, so we unanimously agreed to launch VPI in January.

Building Your Principles

Setting the tone at the outset makes a difference in the long run.

What ideas come to mind for strengthening relationships and/or improving future rollouts in your realm?

How are these ideas organically connected to who you are?

8
The Launch

Sticking to your principles and being there for others can be challenging, especially when it forces uncomfortable issues to the surface. That soon became my dilemma at APP.

> ## Be There for the People
> *Serve the people. Real leadership is servant-leadership.*

By year-end the ducks were lining up pretty well. Although VPI would not launch in earnest until January, I involved APP's clients in the process early on. I created a presentation deck about VPI, and took it on the road. Nancy and I made our first presentation to my boss, Ed Wesley, and to the CS&P Vice President, Terry Lake. We made a similar presentation to leaders of the client organization at Terry's staff meeting.

The presentations introduced Nancy to CS&P's senior leaders and allowed its directors and managers to provide input into the project. I hoped that their participation on the front end would lend credibility to results on the back end. After all, it is hard for people who participate in a project's development to pan the methodology or poo-poo the outcomes later.

Hard, yes. Impossible, no.

Nancy and I interviewed directors, managers, supervisors, and program managers to gain feedback on APP's current performance and suggestions for APP's improvement moving forward. We asked each group a different set of questions designed around their level and type of interaction with APP. In all, we conducted twenty-one interviews.

The results were not encouraging. Although the respondents were not unanimous, a clear majority in each of the four groups had plenty to say about improving APP's operations. By March, Nancy and I summarized their comments. The next step was to communicate those results to the APP management team—not just Roman and Rachel, but client relationship managers, project managers, analysts, and supervisors as well.

The survey was a sensitive issue, so I thought long and hard about how to present it. As a group, APP's self-esteem was low. They believed they were busting their butts for a client organization that failed to respect them, undervalued their work, and (in the case of some clients) wanted to take them over. The APP management team knew their clients were critical of them. They viewed the criticism as unwarranted and unfair, as though the proverbial resident of the glass house was throwing stones.

Nevertheless, they needed to know what was being said about them and their organization. I owed them the truth and the opportunity to burnish their reputation.

Building Your Principles

You have heard the warning "Be careful what you ask for; you just might get it."

How do you respond when doing the right thing creates a new problem, such as negative feedback or hurt feelings?

What is your operative principle for such situations?

How did you (or how will you) develop it?

9
The Feedback

Developing your own principles is commendable; implementing them is mission critical. When it was time to deliver the negative client feedback to the APP team, it would not be all about them. I was their leader and we would take the heat together. My going first was good for the team and provided guidance by way of example.

> ## Be First
> *Model the behavior you expect.*

The meeting to discuss the survey results with my team occurred nearly a year after I arrived to lead the organization. The time lapse had its downside but also allowed me to soften the blow by focusing on my actions rather than other people's.

So, after detailing some of the difficulties we all knew we were having as an organization, I apologized for being slow to lead the organization out of the start-up phase and into its operational phase. "My slowness," I said, "was a major contributor to some of the woes our division faced."

Reviewing the survey results and focusing on myself first required me to display emotional fortitude. I would take the brunt of the clients' comments, so after giving an overview of the feedback, I started with the comments our clients made about leadership (i.e., *me*). I did not mention past leadership or other levels of leadership. I interpreted any comments pertaining to leadership as having been addressed to me and my performance.

In sharing our clients' negative comments about leadership, I committed to taking concrete actions to improve my performance. A Power Point slide with seven essential leadership behaviors from the book *Execution*[25] mapped out my course. The behaviors and their corollaries (my personal to-do list), overlapped almost perfectly with the deficiencies our clients had identified, as the following examples show.

Connecting my leadership behaviors to the clients' comments created a sense of urgency for my suggested next steps.[26] Another essential behavior, "insist on realism,"[27] was a nice entry point for the inherently red-hot discussion about client feedback: I needed to strike a balance between engendering realism and throwing gasoline on the fire.

Thus, I decided not to publish any verbatim comments in print. With one slide, I provided a high-level overview of the survey results. Any specific comments were contained in my voiceovers, and none were attributed to a specific CS&P group.

Despite these measures, the group was glum. People seemed hurt and offended. I knew we could not shrink from the fact that our client organization was asking us to make significant improvements. The "Next Steps" slide I shared with the management team made it abundantly clear that we would face the feedback head-on. The slide's primary bullet points outlined our action plan:

- Report Feedback to Stakeholders

- Incorporate Feedback into Deliverables

- "Deep Dive" into Feedback

IDENTIFIED DEFICIENCY	ESSENTIAL BEHAVIOR
Lack of strong and knowledgeable leadership	"Know your people and your business."
No involvement	Get in "touch with day-to-day realities."
Lack of clear expectations, no vision, no strategy	"Set clear goals and priorities."

Instead of running from the feedback, we were going to share it and incorporate the results into our goals and success measures.

49

With or without the verbatim comments, we would take a cold, hard look at the input received. After the group weathered the initial shock, we would take a deeper dive into survey details. We agreed to a one-day offsite to engage in the robust dialogue that would help us move forward.

But first we retired to our respective corners to lick our wounds.

Building Your Principles

Nobody really wants the recipe for humble pie, but every good leader knows when to eat some.

When has being first been easiest for you?

When has "being last" seemed like a more attractive option? How did you resist its allure?

What spoken or unspoken principle guided you?

How did you discover it, how would you express it in words?

10

Moving Forward

The next stop on the survey-results tour was Ed's office, where Nancy and I met with Ed and Terry Lake, the VP of our client organization. The meeting was our opportunity to summarize our client's feedback in greater detail by providing verbatim comments representative of the survey's common themes, including:

- Improving the processing function;

- Demonstrating the value of APP's systems support and relationship management functions;

- Implementing better communications; and

- Leveraging APP's work ethic.

We had also prepared draft statements regarding APP's responsibilities based on the input we received from our clients. The statements clarified our role, which was to process high-volume, low-risk, non-complex, repetitive work.

Begin with the Purpose in Mind
Ask: What does success look like?

We had previously asked our clients for their definition of *superior value.* The draft value proposition statement we presented at the meeting with Ed and Terry was based on our clients' input. It was succinct: "APP provides efficient, high-volume processing with few errors at a reasonable cost." This was our blueprint of what success looked like.

Nancy and I knew that preparation and transparency would be the necessary hallmarks of our presentation. Therefore, we anticipated the question that officers at any Fortune 200 company would inevitably ask: "So what are you going to do about all of this?"

Ed and Terry did not disappoint. When they popped the question, we responded with a "Next Steps" plan that focused on (1) creating service-level agreements that set forth roles, responsibilities, and performance expectations, (2) finalizing the value proposition statement, and (3) creating a cross- functional team to develop performance metrics.

The vice presidents were pleased. Terry lauded our courage in self-reporting the negative feedback. "I don't think I've seen that before," he said.

We then made a similar presentation at Terry's staff meeting.

It was a bold, courageous move. In essence, we told the key leaders of our client organization that we knew they were displeased with our performance. At the same time, we made a public commitment to meet the expectations they had set for us.

We took another bold and courageous step that was also prudent. During my career I had learned at least two important lessons about surveys: First, don't take a survey unless you are prepared to respond to the results. (That would not be a problem because I commissioned the survey with that idea in mind.) Second, if you want the respondents to know that you value their input, share the survey results with them.

Oh joy.

I presented the results of our survey with the CS&P managers and program managers, in essence declaring that we would turn things around. Not only did I want them to know the results, I wanted them to know that we appreciated them and that we would make good use of the feedback they had given us. I also wrote a memo to the survey respondents. It was candid (honest, truthful, constructive, and objective) and transparent, but also hopeful and encouraging. After the introductory comments I wrote:

"I very much appreciated your candid comments. My candid response is that sometimes it was difficult to hear and to read them. However, I was very encouraged to learn that you believe APP has good people who know how to utilize the resources they have been given. The feedback you provided us has contributed to a value proposition statement in APP and the formation of a cross-functional team that has already recommended new and enhanced performance metrics in APP. Other initiatives and actions, such as an APP performance report card, are underway or planned."

The memo touched on several other points and made clear that we'd gotten the message and were serious about acting on it. I ended the memo by acknowledging that although the feedback was tough news for APP, it would help us "make informed decisions about how best to carry out our responsibilities in a way that provides value to you."

Having shared the survey results with our clients, the APP management team was ready to make informed decisions for the benefit of our clients. We started that process at our one-day offsite.

Building Your Principles

For APP to meet CS&P's expectations for service, we had to understand what providing superior value looked like to them.

What principle helps you, or might help you, to navigate any choppy waters between your organization's current performance and your clients' expectations?

11

The Comeback

We held the offsite at a local hotel. I attended with the rest of APP's management team (Roman, Rachel, the supervisors, project managers, and client relationship managers); Nancy, the VPI project manager; Linda, my project analyst; and the manager of the training organization, Shelly Mercer, who had her own track record of success, was familiar with my identity, and had recommended the formation of APP in the first place.

> ## Involve the People
> *People support only the change they help to create.*

The offsite was to be a hands-on experience, not a recitation of platitudes. Change would begin with all of us, and all of us would support the change we created together. After some opening remarks, I set the context and established our reasons for being there:

- To discuss ideas and assignments as a group, so that we might reach an understanding of where we are going and how we will get there.

- To leave the offsite with a high-level plan of action, and clarity as to its fulfillment.

I provided an update on the Value Proposition Initiative and shared what happened when Nancy and I met with the VPs and Terry's direct reports in CS&P. We revisited the draft value proposition statement: "APP provides efficient, high-volume processing with few errors at a reasonable cost." Instead of cataloguing our failures in meeting the client's expectations, I differentiated between meeting stated goals (which we were doing) and meeting the expectations of others (which we were not). The gap, I explained, was between APP's performance and the *perception* of APP's performance. Settling the question of why we had met goals but not expectations was a far more empowering conversation. To that end, I shared more detailed client feedback; not just for information, but to identify our areas of focus.

Of course, there is a principle for that.

> ## *Begin with the Purpose in Mind*
> *Ask: What does success look like?*

To develop a consensus about what success would mean, I asked the group whether APP needed a purpose statement in addition to the value proposition statement. The answer was decidedly *yes*. The cross-functional team assigned to develop a first draft consisted of Roman, Nancy, one of the client relationship managers, and one of the supervisors.

> ### *Clarify Purpose*
> *Clearly state the purpose, and garner the buy-in you need to succeed.*

After separate break-out sessions and a general session to reach consensus, the group drilled down, deciding that the purpose statement should include five concepts: efficiency, partnership, quality, multiple work streams, and reasonable costs. Clarity of purpose was forming, but we still needed   to ensure group buy-in. So sub-teams formed, with each working on one of the five concepts. Even before a complete statement was developed, agreement was being established.

I was pleased with the group's approach. They were creating change they could support.

To ensure that our clients not only perceived benefit from the purpose statement but also received it, each team specified the partner benefit their assigned concept would produce. So, for example, the sub-team working on *partnership* might list "more timely communications" as the benefit our partners would receive. As our purpose became clearer through participation, we were better able to conceive our desired outcomes, in unity.

The offsite was extremely productive. We concluded by creating an action plan that specified who would do what by when. We had uncovered our comeback road, and we were ready to travel it.

Alas, even the best roads have a pothole or two.

Building Your Principles

The APP offsite was very focused and positive, but beneath the smooth surface, multiple currents flowed. Consensus was critical.

Purpose needed to be crystal clear. Participation was a must. A top-down approach would have been simple, but ineffective.

In similar situations, what principles keep you from taking an easier way out? How do they help those around you to flourish?

12
The Potholes

The group's *esprit de corps* was good as we departed the offsite. Meeting together had engendered a sense of shared identity. Squaring away the performance/perception-of- performance disconnect strengthened the group's confidence and sense of possibility. And leaving the offsite with a concrete action plan generated hope for our future.

Then I went and made a mess of it.

Ironically enough, the matter began with my *Be Trustworthy* principle. It was important for me to be trustworthy, not just with the management team but with everyone in APP. So I behaved, spoke, and engaged in activities that allowed frontline people and me to get to know each other: I established an open-door policy and occasionally ate my lunch in the break room. I served up scoops of deliciousness on Ice-Cream Float Fridays. Every so often, I settled into an empty cubicle among the frontline employees (a habit I'd picked up while leading the training organization).

My efforts succeeded. I established relationships with people from all across the organization, including people who reported to Roman and Rachel.

Perfect...except for the part that wasn't. I inadvertently created the impression that I had given the OK for people to bypass Roman and Rachel and come talk to me instead. That was not my intent. Nevertheless, I masterfully exacerbated the misunderstanding by asking some of my direct reports to pass on messages to Roman and Rachel for me.

Not good, Gregory. Not good at all.

> ### *Be Trustworthy*
> *People follow only leaders they trust; they trust only leaders they know. To become known, leaders must establish relationship.*

Having upended the peace, I created an unscheduled opportunity to embody a key aspect of trustworthiness— when you mess up, you fess up. Rachel was brave enough to point out the negative consequences of my behavior (including how it caused her to feel devalued).

In my personal and written apologies, I made a point of taking ownership and giving Rachel well-deserved praise. A defensive response would have quashed the team's progress in the area of open communications. So I kept it transparent and addressed both sides of the issue I had created. The following is my note to Roman and Rachel, offered *after* I apologized face-to-face:

"I apologize to you for putting you in some difficult situations. I have made it harder for you to trust me by some of my actions. My leadership style includes establishing relationships and trust with everyone on my leadership team, not just my direct reports. This can be a difficult adjustment for direct reports who are new to this style. I have made it a lot worse by my actions.

"Apologies mean little if they don't come with a commitment to make things better. This note represents my commitment to each of you to do better."

I did this in writing, not for repetition's sake, but to make it even easier for them to hold me accountable. I then outlined my commitments to do better in the future:

"First of all, there are things about my leadership style that are important to me. They include interaction with employees at all levels of the organization. I commit to exercising this aspect of my style more appropriately.

"Here's how I propose to do this without damaging trust and while empowering the people around me..."

The memo then described my decision to delegate a responsibility everyone knew was really important to me— making sure that our recognition program reflected our teamwork values.

The hope was that, by entrusting to Rachel something in which I had a personal stake, she would feel more empowered.

How I wish I could say that my *mea culpa* and decision immediately solved the issue. They did not. Helping Roman and Rachel to feel secure in their roles required my focus and intentionality over time. Even so, I'm not sure I ever regained the benefit of the doubt with Rachel.

But there was at least one time when both of them were extremely happy that I was their boss. It involved another big pothole on our comeback road.

> ## Be There for the People
> *Serve the people. Real leadership is servant- leadership.*

This second pothole had some history attached to it. When APP was formed, it inherited processing work from other organizations. One of the programs it took on was designed for high- end customers. After the program was placed under Rachel's management, it became subject to APP's internal auditing procedures, which Roman managed. When an audit revealed substantial errors in the program's enrollment process, both managers came to see me.

Their visit to my office was so far after hours that, as far as we knew, we were the only three people in the building. If the hour did not say enough about the issue's urgency, the fact that both Roman and Rachel were practically shaking did. They promptly explained what had happened and how the errors, which had significant financial and public relations implications, were discovered.

I calmly said, "Explain the errors to me."

They explained, and I asked, "What are the implications?"

They walked me through them.

"We're no longer making those errors, correct?" I asked, still firmly lodged in the calm zone.

"Correct."

"We have the ability to correct past errors, right?"

"Right."

"We can develop a process for making sure they won't happen again, correct?"

"Correct."

Without raising decibel or anxiety levels, I answered, "OK. I'll let our boss know. Meanwhile, let's start working on the remedy."

Their relief was so great that Roman and Rachel burst into laughter. I could hear their minds asking: "What? No emotional outburst? No recriminations? No blame? No panic? You don't want us to go with you to see the boss?"

It turns out that they had spent hours in Roman's office

wondering how to give me the bad news. They thought their careers would be damaged, or over.

I'd like to claim that I'm not one who frets over organizational spilt milk, but my reaction was also heavily influenced by what a former boss modeled when I was party to a huge, high-profile *faux pas*.

The company I was working for had to develop a filing with a regulatory agency. Each business unit created a written submission known as *testimony*. The document explained the firm's request for three years' worth of funding from the regulatory agency. The process was critical to the budget process—so critical that draft testimony was reviewed by company officers and directors.

During my department's review meeting, our vice president presented the written testimony, which resulted from a three-person collaboration. The melding of our minds was not exactly seamless, as the document attested. I will never forget the intensity of the criticism our testimony received. Nor will I forget how our vice president took responsibility for the draft. As heated as the meeting was, she never even looked in our direction.

One outcome of the fiasco was that a consultant was assigned to help me write the next draft. Clearly, the project managers held me accountable for the content and thought I was not up to the task. However, when my vice president explained the decision, she was practically giddy. "This is good news," she declared. "I handpicked the consultant. She knows what she's doing. You'll be writing on your own without two collaborators. You'll be able to shine!"

Thirty-six pages of testimony were streamlined to twelve, and the next draft received rave reviews. I never forgot my VP's support; it taught me how to be there for the people, especially how to support them and not throw them under the bus, so to speak.

When the filing project ended, I exercised my Celebrate the People principle by holding a recognition dinner. I gave my VP the Oh, Yeah. You Get Your Big Brother 'Cause I'll Get My Big Sister and She'll Kick Your Big Brother's Butt Award, commemorating all the support I had received from her during the sometimes contentious process. Clearly, her impact on my career was indelible and led to my providing the same type of support for Roman and Rachel during the enrollment error "crisis."

My VP's handling of my two collaborators was also memorable. They, too, felt the pressure of getting the draft "right" and really wanted to participate in its revision. They contacted me often, hoping to see a draft. But my VP had learned her lesson; she wanted only one cook in that kitchen.

Finally, one of the two collaborators invited me to a meeting with the senior leaders of the project team. He said he "just wanted to get a status," but I sensed that there was more to his invitation. So I received permission from my vice president to bring the second draft for review.

Sure enough, my ex-collaborator skipped the "getting a

status" step and asked to see the draft. The move was not exactly teammate-of-the-year stuff. Yet my vice president continued on the high road. She never responded in kind, but remained cooperative.

> ## *Be Good*
> *More than doing well, we want to do good.*

Years later, with her example in mind, I asked the APP management team to take the high road in working with our client organizations. I told Roman and Rachel, "As we move forward we need to be supportive but not insular. Remain

aware but not fearful. Be responsive but not defensive, confident but not competitive."

I asked them to "immediately engage in behavior that sows the seeds of long-term success" (as in building relationships). Specifically, I asked them to

- increase our credibility by shedding light on every aspect of our operations;

- own up to areas of improvement, without being defensive;

- implement suggestions from our clients and be about their business;

- and assume best intentions (i.e., avoid e-mail wars)."

As a division, we were highly focused on doing well, but we also needed to do good—to honor others, to treat them well, and to keep our intentions right.

My VP had shown me what "doing good" looked like. Now I was showing my team.

I needed to also empower them.

> ## *Empower the People to Do Good*
> *Empowering people to do well is important; encouraging them to do good is important, too.*

Assuming the best intentions of others is not always easy. Becoming offended is much easier. But even this aspect of APP's culture began to turn around. We used a verbatim client comment that described CS&P's view of superior value to sharpen our organizational focus and develop the value proposition statement mentioned earlier.

The client specifically asked for "efficient processing (large volumes in a timely way) with few errors at reasonable costs." We applied this standard to every goal, every new piece of work, and every change made. In each instance, we asked, "Does it relate to cost, quality, or productivity?" If the answer was *no*, we rejected it.

We also implemented an increased focus on performance metrics (we called them *success measures*) and we published them to our clients. This demonstrated that we were cost-, quality-, and productivity-driven, and it allowed our clients to gauge our success in each area.

In addition, we developed the following reports (among others):

- Weekly service-level indicators report for CS&P managers and program managers;

- Monthly reports on each program for executives, managers, and program managers; and

- Daily, weekly, and monthly reports capturing APP's individual and group performance metrics.

Although I held regular meetings with the executive who supervised CS&P's program managers, I relied on Roman and Rachel and the client relationship managers to reset the tone in APP/CS&P relations. I encouraged the managers to schedule more one-on-one meetings. Once or twice I delegated my meeting attendance to Roman or Rachel. This helped to raise their visibility and establish their influence.

Roman and Rachel were empowered to do good. As they embraced the process and as the program managers received regular reports substantiating our support and our mastery of mutually agreed-upon goals, we encountered fewer potholes. We were making fewer errors, the company was spending fewer dollars on our operations, and CS&P's performance was positively impacted.

It became increasingly clear that our clients were pleased with APP's performance. As the division's leader, I was also pleased, and

I appreciated APP's people. They did themselves proud.

Building Your Principles

The best intentions can go awry. When that happens, the temptation to save face is great.

Have you been there? Did you fess up or hunker down?

What principle (or lack thereof) guided your behavior?

13

The People

Mere months into the Value Proposition Initiative I was impressed by the APP management team's willingness to be accountable for its future and to work hard for it. The ultimate success of the organization, however, would depend on the eighty or so frontline people who performed the detailed, day-in-and-day-out processing tasks.

We demanded much from our processors. Even as volume increased, we upped performance metrics, requiring faster processing with fewer errors. We put processors under a microscope, adding individual performance metrics to group metrics, so that each processor's daily, weekly, and monthly performance stats were scrutinized. We also spotlighted them, publicizing (both internally and externally) the group's performance outcomes. Because we shared this data with our clients, they joined us, figuratively speaking, in looking over the processors' shoulders.

We asked all this of our processors even while they worked for someone who did not know their business, at least not at first. When I came on board, I had to learn what they knew, and I had to do it as expeditiously as possible. Two principles played a huge role in making the dynamics work. We have already seen the first one in action. The second one travel travels with it, as shown below.

Be Trustworthy
Be among the People

People follow only leaders they trust; they trust only leaders they know. To become known, leaders must establish relationship.

When I came to lead APP, the people didn't know me and I didn't know them. I set out almost immediately to change that. Before I could ask them to embrace the changes I was initiating (and in some cases, imposing on them), they needed to know me better and to know that I cared about them. As the saying goes, *people don't care how much you know until they know how much you care.* Becoming known to the team was an important step. They soon found out that I was a family man. In fact, I earned big-time points when I brought my twin toddler grandchildren to work one Saturday. They were walking, but still in diapers. If I may say so myself, they were *very* cute.

The three of us made a quick visit so that Linda, my project analyst, could see the kids. The young ladies on the team were very impressed with my diaper-changing skills, and watched attentively as I tended to my grandson's needs. Meanwhile, my granddaughter walked up and down the aisles and made her own set of friends. Needless to say, we made quite a splash that day.

People also discovered (with a lot of help from me) that I love food. I enjoyed Ice-Cream Float Fridays and Taco Thursdays as much as anyone. In all fairness, I was not present *every* time someone in the building opened a pink pastry box. But people seemed to think I was. It wasn't long before folks started leaving goodies on my desk. And whenever anyone brought something special to the break room, somebody made sure I knew about it. All of this made our interaction easy, and over time it generated increasing trust. The years had already taught me that my sense of humor, which showed up in many forums, served as a good icebreaker. At our monthly "all hands" safety meetings I frequently shared on the subject, presented awards, or otherwise recognized deserving team members. My "speaking parts" typically involved humor. My "gags" were known on and off campus. The most memorable was one I pulled on a supplemental worker the day after a picnic. During the outing, brave souls stuck their faces in the cutout of a large cardboard character while the team showed their love by hurling water balloons at them.

Of course, everyone wanted to see the boss get soaked, and someone obliged by landing a balloon square on my nose. The next day, I arrived at the office wearing a bandage to mark the scene of the crime. When someone asked me what happened, I explained that the balloon toss had broken my nose. The news spread like wildfire. We had a near record turnout for our morning aerobics break (a safety initiative), because everybody wanted to see the evidence for themselves. When I fessed up at the end of the break, the place broke out in laughter, and a measure of relief. If anyone believed I was an ole stick-in-the-mud executive, they didn't anymore.

All of this fun supported one of the most important aspects of trustworthiness, which is accessibility. I'm not naïve enough to believe that any of this made me "one of the gang." But being known did make me more approachable, and it freed me to live more among the people than in an ivory tower. My accessibility also required me to be a good listener, often to younger people who were fairly new to the workplace. My listening helped them to figure out "where to go from here."

The rising level of trust softened resistance to the changes established by the VPI. Change is never easy, and it would not be easy at APP. But earning trust also earned me the benefit of the doubt. Even when proposed changes were not readily embraced, they were viewed as having come from a good heart.

There was another significant benefit of "living among the people": it better positioned me to celebrate them, which was also important in changing our organization.

Celebrate the People

We all want to be where we are celebrated, not where we are tolerated.

Being celebrated at work is not just a feel-good thing; it is genuinely and deeply affirming. This is important to people, so we spent a lot of time doing it, particularly by recognizing and rewarding folks. During the same month we launched the Value Proposition Initiative, we also (coincidentally) launched the APP recognition program. It took some doing, but overcoming the hurdles was well worth the effort.

My thought was simple: if we were going to recognize people, we needed to recognize *all* of them when those rewards were earned. If all of the people are doing the work but only some are rewarded, the rest feel cheated and those being recognized feel guilty. But because 50 percent of APP's workforce were contract workers receiving paychecks from TWS, and because there were legal and liability implications for treating them like TCS employees, there

Empower the People to do Good

Empowering people to do well is important; encouraging them to do good is important, too.

were obstacles to rewarding 100 percent of the people.

We overcame this hurdle by involving the management of TWS. I was very grateful that they agreed to recognize their employees as well. It was good for the whole team.

Once we overcame the recognition hurdle, I assigned an executive sponsor to be our roadblock buster. The sponsor assembled a team of frontline employees and tasked them with developing the recognition program. What a wonderful job they did! The program asked employees to nominate a peer or a peer team for recognition. APP winners received prize points redeemable in the company's recognition program; TWS winners received cash awards.

In addition to formal recognition, I made it a point to personally express my gratitude for people's hard work when I visited each manager's staff or recognition meetings. There I thanked the entire group, making sure my comments were specific and personal—not just empty platitudes, but meaningful, relatable remarks.

The approach I sought was a balanced one. As focused as we became and as hard as we worked, I acknowledged that work life was not all about work. Even when recognizing people's accomplishments, we did it in fun ways. You know what they say about *all work and no play*.

> ## Create Work/Life Balance for the People...Even at Work
>
> *We work to live; we don't live to work. It's OK to be intentional about having fun at work. Ice-Cream Float Fridays, anyone?*

Ice-Cream Float Fridays and Taco Thursdays were fun on so many levels. They broke up the routine of 8-to-5 workdays. Plus, root beer, cola, and orange floats were the perfect hot-weather treat. And, because managers scooped all the ice cream and poured all the sodas, employees discovered how it felt to be served by their bosses. Both groups relished the experience, and it gave the managers a fun way to express their gratitude.

Such activities also generated a blissfully egalitarian atmosphere. Walls come down when people are chatting and trying to fish blobs of ice cream out of their sodas without splashing pop all over themselves or plopping the scoops onto the floor. It was a great environment for everyone getting to know everyone else. We were especially blessed in being the only work group in our building. This allowed us to hold interactive events such as cubicle-decorating contests without disturbing any other organizations. Contests were particularly popular. Each had a theme, and each section of the building had a winner. These activities broke up the monotony and made for a workplace that was serious, but also lots of fun.

We were so intent about creating a work/life balance that we formed a Fun Team of primarily frontline employees, with me in their midst. Management participated, not as proverbial feudal lords "allowing" the serfs to "have their fun," but as real people joining in the festivities.

One of our legendary holiday events involved karaoke. The first half of the day was all business and opened with a report on safety, the company's top priority. The presentation ran long and was mind-numbingly detailed. Given the circumstances, it dampened expectations for the fun ahead. But when the safety segment ended, I took the stage and launched into Aretha Franklin's "(You Make Me Feel Like) A Natural Woman."[28] The sights and sounds shocked and delighted the group. Levity was restored and the boss proved he wasn't an old fogy.

That was all the crowd needed to get their party on.

Yeah, we worked hard. But we played hard, celebrated hard, and recognized hard. Therefore, we didn't mind hard work. Signs of growth were cropping up. As Roman and Rachel grew into their roles, they took on even greater responsibilities and led this hard-working group into even higher levels of success.

Building Your Principles

Being among the people is not a risk-free endeavor.

Transparency and relationship require a level of humility that is, well, humbling.

Do you prefer the comfort of your corner office or are you willing to breach your "safe place"?

Do you have a principle for that? How is it working for you?

14

Pulling It All Together

From the moment APP's management team emerged from its April offsite, it began forging a new future for the organization. That was exactly the right approach. From that day forward, it would not be up to me, but up to them.

> ## Be an Enabler (Empower Good People to Do Good Work)
> *Do not micromanage.*

As I explained to the managers, my role was to set the direction, establish clear parameters within which to operate, and let the management team do what they did best. If needed, I would bust through any roadblock that hindered their success, and I would support them with our leadership and our clients.

To empower Rachel and Roman and help them feel more comfortable in their expanding roles, I shared some pointers on how to relate with me. The tips provided context for our respective functions and ways to proceed when the way seemed uncertain. Here are some of the insights I offered:

"One of the primary reasons I'm here is to help you succeed.

- Please elevate issues when necessary.

- Don't hesitate to give me an assignment that helps you get the job done.

"You report to me, but you're in charge of the APP organization now, not me. Shelly is an excellent role model and knows how to strike this balance. You might want to establish a peer mentoring relationship with her."

Shelly knew firsthand how willing I was to support her as the leader of the Frontline Training Organization (FTO). She was on the tail end of an incident that was uncharacteristic of me but affirmed my desire to support her. The incident made the rounds as concrete evidence that "Greg has our backs. It began one afternoon with a call from my boss. He had just returned from his boss's staff meeting. There he learned that the manager of a company-wide systems implementation project had unloaded negative feedback about FTO's performance. Initially, I was flabbergasted, knowing that a decision had been made (at the corporate level) to have frontline employees train their peers on the new system. However, many of those "lay trainers" were not being released by their supervisors to perform the training or were not confident enough in their own training ability to accept training assignments.

The FTO trainers stepped in to cover for the lay trainers who missed their assignments for the reasons stated. When lay trainers did show up, they performed like the inexperienced trainers they were. The initiative was not being executed very well.

When the project leader gave her assessment, she lumped together experienced FTO trainers with "lay trainers," claiming that FTO trainers were often failing to show up and were not performing well when they did. She effectively punished them for trying to salvage a situation created at the corporate level and unfairly foisted upon frontline groups.

As I listened, my disbelief turned to anger in no time flat. Up till that point in my corporate history, my cuss-free language made me stand out in the culture. But on that day, I vigorously refuted the report, called it "crap," and added (to my own amazement) that it was "bullsh*t!"

I'm pretty sure I heard my boss laughing on the other end, as he thought, "What? Greg just used a cuss word!"

I gave him an earful explaining that FTO trainers were not only showing up for their assignments, but also for the lay trainers' assignments. I shared an example of one trainer volunteering to accept a last-minute request for four hours on a Saturday morning—

even though her bridal shower was scheduled for later that day.

My boss expressed his support and assured me that the truth would find its way to the surface. It did little to change my mood. Coincidentally, I was scheduled to meet with Shelly and one of FTO's project managers after the call. By the time they arrived some thirty minutes later, I was still fuming and unable to sit still. So we walked around the building while I explained what happened.

I *know* they laughed at me, or more correctly, with me. They were so tickled, we barely talked about the reason for my outburst. First, they were shocked that I would use a cuss word in a conversation with our vice president. Second, they were pleased that I had done so in support of their friends and colleagues. Mr. Calm, Cool, and Collected had become a firebrand on their behalf. That may be slightly exaggerated, but as far as they were concerned, I was the boss who had their backs, even with *his* boss.

For FTO and APP managers, this was extremely empowering. FTO managers were already extroverts on steroids. For them the incident meant a change in *mind-set* along the lines of "I'm will continue to be assertive, but at least I know Greg will have my back." For APP managers, it contributed to a change in *behavior*, as in "I will be assertive because I know Greg has my back." Both outcomes were positive for the organization.

The incident increased Roman and Rachel's comfort level in developing new ideas, such as creating lead positions, reaching out to CS&P program managers to solve relational challenges, and making business cases for additional positions. Their confidence grew so much that I was completely at ease placing them in a potentially nerve- wracking situation.

The firm's Chief Executive Officer and Chairman of the Board, Craig Purdue, had established the personal goal of meeting with every organization in the company. In September, 2010, he would meet with FTO and APP. While most organization heads took the lead in presenting to Mr. Purdue and in conducting tours of their facilities, I took a different approach: I asked my managers to host him.

There was no doubt that FTO managers would be confident presenters; but I was not as sure about Roman and Rachel. The scathing remarks from their clients had left fresh wounds mere months earlier. Although no one was directly named, Roman and Rachel were clearly targeted by the criticism. Their growth in confidence since then was very apparent, but it was not exactly sky-high, and this was a big step up.

To their immense credit, Roman and Rachel owned the opportunity. They made their presentations with confidence and they led the APP facility tour with pride. They chose accountability and they became powerful in the choosing. With their power they led their organization's growth so ably that it hardly resembled the one I'd been appointed to lead the previous year.

Focus on Purpose

If you chase two rabbits, both will escape.

One of their winning ways was to adopt, as a team, my mantra of focusing on cost, quality, and productivity, the key elements of APP's value proposition statement. Their strong focus paid off.

Focusing on purpose means "keeping the main thing the main thing." This principle naturally overlaps with the idea of aligning everything with purpose, but it all starts with getting "the main thing" settled. Our focus was cost, quality, and productivity. With that established, we deselected all rabbit trails and actively sought new ways of concentrating our efforts on the job at hand.

One of the balancing acts already mentioned was to keep enough processors on hand to efficiently handle workload spikes without over-inflating labor costs. The solution we crafted was to create a group of generalists, processors who were skilled in multiple programs. When a particular program ramped up, the generalists could easily switch over to help with the increased volume. This eliminated the need to keep "extra" processors on any given program "just in case" demand surged.

We also borrowed a tactic from TCS's call center and created daily performance metrics to track error rates for each work group and, as mentioned earlier, for each processor. The metrics were not used to punish, but to highlight opportunities for additional training. They also helped identify our strongest performers, who then became candidates for the generalist positions.

> ## *Align Everything with Purpose*
> *Be sure your people, resources, performance metrics, etc. are compatible with your goals.*

Once we centered on our purpose, it was easy to align everything else with it. Our budget, goals, performance metrics, and even key management decisions became laser focused.

APP's goals for 2010 had been developed prior to the Value Proposition Initiative, and it showed. Out of eight goals, only one pertained to performing work for clients. No wonder the client survey was so negative! Once cost, quality, and productivity became APP's focal points, the organization's goals changed *dramatically*.

For example, of our six goals in 2011, one was a safety goal, three related directly to the areas our clients cared about most (cost and quality), the fifth goal supported a client's marquee program (by improving customer satisfaction), and the sixth supported a business unit mandate to develop a 2014 customer strategy.

APP's 2011 budget request also lined up with the organization's stated goals. Seventy-five percent of the additional dollars requested were tied to the growth of client programs. The other 25 percent would fund system changes dictated by the company's implementation of an enterprise resource program.

By focusing on APP's primary purposes and aligning its goals and resources accordingly, the management team positioned the organization for even greater success. It was a satisfying endeavor for everyone.

Seeing team members enjoy the fruits of their success was particularly sweet for me, because they had no one to credit but themselves.

Building Your Principles

What closely-held value—from your upbringing, belief system, education, or experiences—empowers you to empower others, especially when "having their backs" exposes your own?

How might verbalizing it be helpful to you and others?

15

They Did Good Work, Themselves

I love it when the people I lead achieve their definition of success. A big part of my management style is to position people to succeed, give them what they need to succeed, and give them the elbow room to excel at what they do best.

Naturally, opinions sometimes differ about what people need to be successful, as they did when, for developmental reasons, I implemented a job swap between APP's middle managers. I asked Roman, who managed the client support function, and Rachel, who managed the operations function, to trade places. They did not exactly embrace the idea. But I believed the swap would help each of them grow. The bonus would be the potential benefit to the organization and our clients. Roman was more gregarious by nature. That would be a good fit for interacting with processors on the front line. Their work was often monotonous and our "play hard" approach to combatting monotony and maintaining high performance would be turbocharged by someone with Roman's charisma.

Rachel was not as outgoing as Roman, but her analytical mind was ideal for a group tasked with client relationship functions, as well as systems and technical support for APP's clients. My goal was to give both managers a place to flourish, and to benefit their respective groups in the process.

> ## Be an Enabler (Empower Good People to Do Good Work)
> Do not micromanage.

We saw the *Be an Enabler* principle in action when managers were empowered because I had their backs. The swap was a different kind of case. For Roman and Rachel, recognizing the benefits of my actions was not so easy. But as my rollout made clear, they were the primary beneficiaries. I laid out my rationale in a memo:

"I believe job rotation offers huge benefits to the manager who is rotating, to the organization where the manager is rotating, and to the manager's own organization upon his or her return. With that in mind, I am announcing the six- month job rotation of Rachel Williams and Roman Anderson.

"I wholeheartedly support Rachel's and Roman's development as leaders. I also expect APP to benefit from the broader perspectives they will bring back to their respective jobs."

You'll remember that when I first arrived, Roman and Rachel saw themselves as being anything but empowered. The job swap was an attempt to change that by increasing their managerial skill sets. I also supported them with personal encouragement and with latitude to manage based on their individual leadership styles. The last thing I wanted was for them to parrot my style, or worse, to defer to me and suppress their own visibility as leaders and managers.

You might also remember that I shared tips on how to meet my expectations, emphasizing that even though Roman and Rachel reported to me, they were in charge of the APP organization. My intent was to encourage their assertiveness and creativity, and to have them put me to work helping them. In case that did not show my confidence in them, I also said, "This is your organization."

I am pleased to say that Roman and Rachel responded to the encouragement, proceeded as empowered managers, and produced good work. Not only did the culture change for the better, but improvements were documented. The following statistics highlight APP's progress, by way of comparison between *Then* (early client feedback and other painful realities on the ground) and *Now* (corresponding client comments and updated statistics). The first category consists of verbatim client quotes that Nancy and I shared with Ed (my VP) and Terry (the clients' VP) at the beginning of the Value Proposition Initiative. The second category includes comments from the presentation we made to the two vice presidents at the end of the Value Proposition Initiative. The comparison shows the growth of APP's people. By and large, they themselves did the good work of improving the organization.

CLIENT FEEDBACK THEN	CLIENT FEEDBACK AND DATA NOW
"I don't want the processing function, but I don't want to worry about it either."	Clients are considering transferring additional work to APP.
"APP's biggest weaknesses are its costs, its management, and the lack of quality controls."	Volume increased 4.6%. Productivity increased 15%. Error rate percentage decreased by 32%. Average cost per application decreased 36%.
"I don't see the value of APP's systems support and relationship management functions."	"Seeking a centralized view of program enrollment."
	"[APP's client relationship managers are] working with stakeholders to develop a centralized strategy."
	"Adding centralized program enrollment view to CRM, credit card program enrollment, and self-service strategy work [by working with APP's systems support group]."

These results and others strongly indicated that two really good managers were turned loose to do what they do best in the way they thought best, were supported along the way, and produced really excellent results, as our clients' *Now* comments attest.

As thrilled as I was with APP's good work, I was also proud that our group did good. More on that, in the next chapter.

16
They "Did Good," Too

Our work hard, play hard philosophy was activated in meaningful ways by the processors and analysts on the front lines. The management team asked them to take lead roles and we empowered the managers and frontline workers by supporting their decisions, not just when we agreed with them, *but even when we didn't.*

Provided their decisions did not violate a law, policy, or sound business practice, we did not override the judgment of frontline employees. We did ask them to implement ideas in ways consistent with our group's values (i.e., our principles). And yes, we shared our wisdom with them explaining, for example, that if you put out a suggestion box, you must be prepared to respond to each suggestion. Beyond that, we encouraged them to take ownership of doing good.

Empower the People to Do Good

Empowering people to do well is important; encouraging them to do good is important, too.

Freshly empowered, the frontline employees helped the organization do good. They developed and operated the recognition program already discussed. They led the safety incentive program. They formed and operated the Fun Team. They led *ad hoc*, just-for-the-fun-of-it activities, including our renowned cubicle decoration contests and sports days.

Having fun and breaking up the monotony of repetitive tasks was important, but playing hard produced other valuable results. Not only was there an increased sense of teamwork, but also a heightened awareness of being in relationship with one another. Having the building to ourselves was very helpful in this regard because it allowed us to create an unbounded sense of community.

This was reflected in our 2011 Work Atmosphere Survey (WAS) results. This annual survey was company-wide, taken by employees at all levels. The graphics shown below reflect the people who responded "somewhat agree" or "strongly agree" to the questions posed. I received combined (APP and FTO) results for the Processing and Training Services group (PATS). Both organizations did good work and good things overall.

Out of twenty-three categories, PATS exceeded overall division results in twenty. Although our excellent results regarding work quality (Performance Excellence, Customer people principles.

APP did well in every area we had targeted for improvement. The data points below cover several areas in which PATS exceeded CFO's results. I've organized the stats under the people principles our group had embraced.

PRINCIPLE: CELEBRATE THE PEOPLE		
Topic	CFO	PATS
Recognition	67%	76%
Growth and Development	73%	78%

PRINCIPLE: INVOLVE THE PEOPLE		
Topic	CFO	PATS
Overall Engagement	90%	95%
Diversity or Inclusion	81%	89%

PRINCIPLE: BE AMONG THE PEOPLE		
Topic	CFO	PATS
Teamwork	70%	71%
Immediate Supervisor	78%	81%

PRINCIPLE: CREATE WORK/LIFE BALANCE FOR THE PEOPLE…EVEN AT WORK		
Topic	CFO	PATS
Work/Life Balance	76%	89%
Job Satisfaction	76%	84%

PRINCIPLE: EMPOWER THE PEOPLE TO DO GOOD		
Topic	CFO	PATS
Respect	70%	76%
Integrity	75%	79%
Ethics	78%	79%

These results were generated largely by employees who felt empowered to make a difference. And make a difference they did. They did not need their leader to breath down their necks or control their every move. They needed to be unleashed to do their best and become their best. One of my favorite quotes about leadership is from Lao Tzu: "A leader is best when people barely know he exists…when his work is done, his aim fulfilled, they will say: 'We did it ourselves."[29]

The leader's role is to invite the team to own center stage. Because I was *among the people*, APP employees never felt abandoned. But my presence was guided by the five people principles that helped me motivate them to do their best. They responded and accomplished our goals. Because they were at their best, I shared their sense of accomplishment.

As Ed said on countless occasions, "It's all about leadership." I would tweak his maxim ever so slightly: "It's because of *being* a leader, which is all about identity."

Being a Leader

17

Leading Out of My Own Identity

One of the American leaders I most admire is General Colin Powell. He's smart, direct, tough, and compassionate. Yet, if I studied his every move and emulated him "to a T," it would not make me an admired leader in my own right.

Much of American leadership training revolves around imitation. My question is, "How's that working out?" In Barbara Kellerman's words, "If Americans are so good at developing leaders, why is America in such a mess? Can those of us in the leadership industry honestly say that, in the last several decades, we have had the impact we wanted and intended?"[30]

In my opinion, we still have some ground to cover.

Is it possible that the industry's impact has been limited by the mistaken belief that we can become the leaders we admire by emulating their key traits? Do we lack impact because "[t]he debate about leadership skills/characteristics/ style, suggests something permanent can exist and be possessed by a person appointed to the task."[31] I do not believe that leadership is something to be grasped, but a process we engage based on personal identity and our ways of relating to others.

As leaders developing ourselves and future leaders, we can have a greater impact by viewing leadership training through the lens of this relational and identity-based dynamic. We would do well to quit copying the traits touted in seminars and books and instead focus on the larger and more important awareness and development of individual identity and the principles that issue from it.[32]

In other words, we should focus on leadership as a dynamic process that involves personal reflection and self-development[33] and results in the formation of a leadership identity. This is the process of growing into better versions of ourselves. According to Karp and Helgø, this process "[b]egins with understanding the story of leaders' lives. Leaders' images from the past are a function of how they may learn and develop from their life story. It is a matter of framing life stories that allow leaders to see themselves not as passive observers of their lives but as individuals who have developed self-awareness from important experiences."[34] They suggest focusing on the following questions:

"What are the leaders' stories? What knowledge and

experiences [do they] have? What are their unique strengths, skills and capabilities?

"Who have they met who has inspired them, who has challenged them, and who has contributed to their development as human beings and as leaders?

"What is their network or team of supportive people, possible mentors and advisors? What are the leaders' family backgrounds, their interests, and their roots of origin?

"What challenges and difficult experiences have they overcome and how can they use these difficulties to give meaning to their life? How do they find motivation from these difficult experiences and how do they grow from these?"[35]

This is a darn good description of how I developed the fifteen principles I used in leading the Application and Payments Processing group. Ironically enough, I would add one more important source: the leadership industry. One of my principles resulted from my attendance at a leadership seminar (though it came from a participant rather than an instructor). Several other principles were gleaned from leadership books and adopted, adapted, or otherwise personalized.

There is an important point I haven't yet mentioned: the fifteen principles I covered are not my complete set. They are the subset of principles I used most during my APP assignment. I have not used the same constellation at any other time in the past, and mostly likely will not in the future.

For example, in my most recent leadership assignment, the five organizational principles that were so successful at APP failed miserably. APP benefitted from principles focused on purpose; the focus of my recent assignment was emotional intelligence and management. It was a different assignment in a different culture. You could say the organization had its own identity. So I adjusted and relied on different organizational principles.

Are you getting the picture? Just as you are not me and I am not you, your most recent assignment is not like your next one. With that in mind, let's talk about how you can develop your principles, not as a static group, but as a pool you can draw from as needed.

18

Leading Out of Your Own Identity

By now it is clear that this is not a "How to Be a Leader Like Me" book. The leadership assignment I recounted was not offered as a model to be replicated, but a real-life (sometimes painfully real) example of leading out of one's identity. Thankfully, the story ended well. But it wasn't always pretty, as you know. I got some important things right and had my share of blunders. But always, I relied on principles that reflect who I am and am still becoming.

As Karp and Helgø explain: "[L]eaders create their identities as their individual and personal ways to leadership. Discovering individual ways to leadership requires a commitment to develop one's self."[36] The commitment involves, not the appropriation of someone else's model, but a process of becoming fully acquainted with the person in the mirror.

If leadership is about identity (and I believe it is), a critical component of our development as leaders is to build leadership models that are unique to, and compatible with, the individuals we are. A quote shared in the Prologue so perfectly echoes my reasons for writing this volume that it bears repeating:

"We feel it is important to emphasize that no one right way exists to be an effective, dynamic captain.... The ultimate goal of this book is that you use it as a reference or guide in constructing your own Captain's Handbook. Feel free to develop your own notes and definition that apply to you, your coaches, and your team. Add your own ideas and perspectives, and then pass it down to future captains. This way, you can leave your own legacy."[37]

Likewise, *this* book is best used as a point of reference or a guide in building *your own* leadership principles. Hopefully, as you read each page, you "ate the meat and discarded the bones." As you consider the implications to your leadership journey, develop *your own* concepts, the ones that apply to you and those you lead. Add *your own* thoughts and points of view. Then pass your principles down to future leaders who will pick and choose and adapt and adopt them according to *their* identities. That's a great way to leave *your* legacy.

Where to Begin

If you were to set aside several minutes right now, you could no doubt think of principles you rely upon to lead your organization. Some may be unspoken rules by which you live and lead. Others may be concepts you have consciously verbalized. As they come to mind now, jot them down. You will need to add some intentionality and sustained reflection to round out your list. But in a short time, you will develop a solid, useful set of principles.

This is not about rules. Your principles are grist for your leadership mill. They can guide you, help you avoid pitfalls, and ensure a consistency to your leadership and your organization's culture. But if they exist in a vacuum, disconnected from who you are, they are mere legalisms. For your principles to "have legs" they must be the product of your identity. When you *know who you are* you will know what your principles are.

How well do you know yourself? How willing are you to find out? "The forming of leadership identity is a result of hard work related to the understanding and development of oneself in relation to others."[38] With that in mind, reflect on your life and consider the

- lessons you have learned from parents, caregivers, mentors, and advisors;

- challenges you have overcome and the meaning they give to your life;

- uniqueness that is you, including the knowledge you possess and the experiences you have had;

- people who have contributed to your development as a human being and a leader; and

- concepts you have adopted from leadership seminars and books.

As you reflect on these items, you will bump into principles that have been operating in the background of your life. Don't look for them to ooze profundity. So-called simple truths have a profound impact, if you apply them.

Building Your Principles

It is easy to value the ideas that "famous people" share, and dismiss your own. Have you discounted your life lessons? If so, push past any insecurities about what you have to offer. Don't let your legacy leave this earth with you. Which seemingly insignificant principles deserve another look, right here, right now?

Lessons Learned in Your Upbringing

Throughout your formative years, family, caregivers, teachers, coaches, and others taught life lessons that helped shape your character and your ways. Whether or not you are consciously aware of them, they guide you even now. By reflecting, you can pull them out of the "ether" and into your conscious thoughts. Then you can become more intentional in relying on them to guide your leadership. Remember that simple ideas can have very deep implications.

For example, most of us were taught to "play nice." If that sounds like a no-brainer, consider what would happen if *Play Nice* became a teamwork principle. Would your team selection process change? Might it cause you to proceed more carefully instead of rushing to fill the need and possibly slighting someone? How would you assign work? Would playing nice make it harder to play favorites? What if a dispute surfaced? Would you justify avoiding confrontation and/or wearing your emotions on your sleeve? Or, would "play nice" compel you to own up, hold your temper, and facilitate resolution?

Reflect on how you were raised. Your past is a treasure trove of principles.

Building Your Principles

Many personal principles are developed in the crucible of painful events. Some of them are unconsciously shelved because they are attached to difficult memories. Can you pull one or two off the shelf and jot them down now? How might doing so redeem the loss you suffered and benefit of others?

Lessons Learned in "The School of Hard Knocks"

You already know about some of my glaring missteps, like the time I inadvertently undermined the authority of Roman and Rachel at the exact point in time when I was working to earn their trust. That was a "beaut," as they say.

My principles are solid, but I'm imperfect. One ugly mistake I am loath to make is to pass along comments from those who want to remain anonymous. I have, however, done that very thing. When I did, it absolutely (but thankfully only temporarily) ruined a working relationship with a colleague. It happened during a midterm performance evaluation, of all places. This was a new working relationship and, because I was not well known by the person, I had not yet earned the trust needed to credibly communicate such comments.

Enter The (merciless) School of Hard Knocks, which permanently engraved this principle on my psyche: Avoid passing anonymous comments to the subject of those comments, no matter how constructive those comments might be.

Lest you chuckle too heartily at my foolishness, search your archives for the lessons you learned at The School. Turn them into principles, and you will avoid future visits to your "alma mater."

Building Your Principles

Consider your most recent mistake. What did it cost you? How did it affect others? What lesson(s) did you learn? Put it (them) in simple words that briefly summarize the idea. You're building your principles!

Stories You Rely on to Make a Point to Others

This book used a story to make a point. You have stories that can be of value to others. Become cognizant of them. Use them appropriately to help others. Stories are more powerful than finger-pointing; they slip past our defenses and defy our preconceived notions. They help us to apply beneficial ideas to real life.

A certain story has helped me keep my head straight many times. It is low on drama, but high on wisdom—and it is *so simple*. It began when I prepared a written reprimand for an employee in my work group. When my boss reviewed the memo, he said, "I know this will make you feel better, but it is not helpful."

He was spot on. My point was strong and accurate. But helpful it was not. My boss's advice produced a personal principle that has kept me out of trouble countless times: *Don't let your emotions get in the way of being constructive.* Now, whenever someone seeks my advice on how to handle a similar situation, I share the story. It shows that I understand their temptation. It also shows that, if I can make the right choice in spite of my feelings, they can, too.

Get a handle on your stories and tell them. Turn them into principles and use them.

Building Your Principles

You have stories to tell. How might they help in your family, your workplace, in moments of crisis? How might a simple story make it easier for someone you know to step higher? Make some notes. Build some principles. Share your stories. That's leadership.

What You Have Learned from Bosses and Mentors

I worked my way through college in the sports department of a major metropolitan newspaper. Our goal each night was to produce a perfect paper. Every morning the editors read through every word and statistic to ensure accuracy. Whenever a mistake was found, the editor would say aloud for everyone to hear, "There goes our perfect paper."

Perfection was perhaps an impossible standard, but it kept us on our toes. One of the sports department's key players (no pun intended) reminded us often that "it never hurts to check." I embraced the idea and have adopted it as a principle. If I have the slightest doubt about something, I check one more time, even if doing so seems overboard.

What were some of your bosses' mantras? Mentally scan your career history, jot down their favorite ideas and adopt the ones that fit your identity. Building your principles is easier than you think.

Building Your Principles

Think about that boss who got under your skin, but taught you some valuable lessons. Which ones can you adopt or adapt or somehow make your own—not because they are good ideas, but because they resonate for you as a leader? What does your version of them look like, and how might they impact current or future assignments?

What You Glean from Seminars and Books

Having attended day-long and week-long leadership seminars I can attest that they are always jam-packed with information, revelation, and inspiration. Yet, I rarely remember more than 10 percent of the content. I do, however, strive to come away with two or three "nuggets" that I can put into practice.

The same applies to leadership books. I have read many, from pamphlets to tomes. The "nugget rule" applies here, too. One of my favorite nuggets is attributed to Peter Drucker: "[Y]ou can put your boots in the oven, but that don't make them biscuits."[39] Here's my translation: "Labels don't redefine actions." A pay cut is pay cut. Don't try to call it something else when communicating it to the troops. I have adopted this nugget as a personal principle. It has affected my interaction, integrity, and credibility. Boots ain't biscuits, and I won't pretend they are. When "boots" are coming their way, I say so.

There are many seasoned leaders with a wealth of information to share. Not everything in their books and seminars will fit you like a glove. But there are more than enough golden nuggets to go around. So start cherry-picking. It's a great way to build your principles.

Building Your Principles

Have you read stacks of leadership books and articles

and attended countless seminars? If you are anything like me, you have forgotten 90 percent of what you learned, but not necessarily forever. Cash in on your investment. Pull a couple of books off the shelf and browse. Find two or three or ten nuggets that speak to you and write them down, in your own words. Which ones can help you today?

Use Your Principles Well

These are just a few of the rich depositories you can mine for principles that express your leadership identity. You don't have to reinvent the wheel, but you cannot roll exactly like the next person. Find the ideas that reflect who you are and adapt them as needed. But remember that they won't all work for every assignment. Treat your set of principles the way you would a good toolbox: use the tools you need for the task at hand. Every assignment is different. Every work group has different needs. What worked perfectly at your last assignment could be anathema to your next one.

Building Your Principles

How does your "toolbox" look? Which "tools" can you use right now? Which ones do you need to add to your complete set? Put your life lessons to work. They are invaluable.

Final Thoughts

My primary goal throughout these pages has been to free you from trying to be someone you are not and invite you to be the *one and only amazing you*, a leader in your own right. May this book empower you to do good work, and to simply do good. May you come to know yourself better by learning from your life stories, developing a strong sense of identity, building your personal leadership principles, and successfully leading and mentoring others.

May you use the appropriate principles in the appropriate ways at the appropriate times to produce results that benefit all. And may you enjoy the ultimate success that comes from being the real you.

That is a legacy of which you can be proud.

ENDNOTES

1 Eilene Zimmerman, "Jeffrey Pfeffer: Why the Leadership Industry Has Failed," Stanford Graduate School of Business, https://www.gsb.stanford.edu/insights/ jeffrey-pfeffer-why-leadership-industry-has-failed, accessed January 8, 2016.

2 Barbara Kellerman, *The End of Leadership* (New York: Harper Business, 2012), Kindle edition, introduction.

3 Ibid.

4 Ibid.

5 Indiana High School Athletic Association, *Captain's Handbook*, http:// www.ihsaa.org/portals/0/ihsaa/documents/membership/capt ains%20handbook.pdf, accessed December10, 2015; emphasis added.

6 Kellerman, *The End of Leadership*, Kindle edition, introduction.

7 Juliette Fairley, "Natural Leader Shares Secrets for the Rest of Us," review of *The Leadership Secrets of Colin Powell*, by Oren Harari, *USA Today*, March 10, 2002, Business Books, http://usatoday30.usatoday.com/money/moneybooks/ 2002-03-11-powell-leadership.htm, accessed January 8, 2016.

8 I want to distinguish leadership training from skills training (e.g., training in better communication, managing change, leveraging technology, etc.). The latter is not the focus of this book.

9 Derek, customer review of *Nice Guys Finish First*, by Doug Sandler, Amazon.com, May 19, 2015, http://www.amazon.com/gp/customer-reviews/ R2JMQZBVFSUPQ7/ref=cm_cr_pr_viewpnt? ie=UTF8&ASIN=162865161X#R2JMQZBVFSUPQ7,

accessed December 10, 2015. The customer's dismay does not diminish the book's usefulness, but helps to explain why *identity* is essential in leadership.

10 Identity is defined as "a multidimensional construct [or concept] used throughout social sciences to describe an individual's comprehension of him or herself as a discrete, separate entity." Thomas Karp and T. I. Helgø, "Leadership as Identity Construction: The Act of Leading People in Organisations; A Perspective from the Complexity Sciences," *Journal of Management Development,* 28, no. 10 (2009), 884.

11 Ibid., 892.

12 Ibid., 884.

13 Ibid.

14 In order to be constructively candid about my experiences, I have changed certain details and used pseudonyms to protect the innocent, the guilty, and myself!

15 "Peter F. Drucker > Quotes," Goodreads.com, https://www.goodreads.com/ author/quotes/12008.Peter_F_Drucker?page=2, accessed December 12, 2015.

16 Macmillandictionary.com, s.v. "principle," http:// www.macmillandictionary.com/dictionary/british/principle, accessed December 12, 2015;   emphasis added.

17 "Albert Einstein > Quotes > Quotable Quote," goodreads.com, http:// www.goodreads.com/quotes/7275-in-the-middle-of-difficulty-lies-opportunity, accessed December 29, 2015.

18 Larry Bossidy and Ram Charan, *Execution* (New York: Crown Business, 2002), 23.

19 Stephen R. Covey, *7 Habits of Highly Effective*

People: Powerful Lessons in Personal Change, 25th anniversary ed. (RosettaBooks, 2013), Kindle edition, pt. 2, sec. 2.

20 I first recall hearing this concept from John Maxwell, but it is ubiquitous. As organizational behavior expert Margaret Wheatley explains, "For the past fifty years a great bit of wisdom has circulated in the field of organizational behavior: People support what they create." Margaret J. Wheatley, *Finding Our Way: Leadership for an Uncertain Time* (San Francisco: Berrett-Koehler, 2007), 110

21 Covey, *7 Habits*, Kindle edition, pt. 2, sec. 2.

22 This and other classic John Wooden principles are covered in *Be Quick—But Don't Hurry! Finding Success in the Teachings of a Lifetime* (New York: Simon & Schuster, 2001), written by Andrew Hill, with John Wooden.

23 James C. Collins and Jerry I. Porras, *Built to Last: Successful Habits of Visionary Companies* (New York: Harper Business, 2002).

24 George Labovitz and Victor Rosansky, *The Power of Alignment: How Great Companies Stay Centered and Accomplish Extraordinary Things* (Wiley & Sons, 1997).

25 Bossidy and Charan, *Execution*, 57.

26 Thank you, John P. Kotter for your book, *A Sense of Urgency* (Boston: Harvard Business School, 2008).

27 Bossidy and Charan, *Execution*, 57

28 Gerry Goffin, Carole King, and Gerald Wexler, "(You Make Me Feel Like) A Natural Woman," © EMI Music Publishing, vocal performance by Aretha Franklin on the album, *Lady Soul*, Atlantic Records. Originally released 1968.

29 "Lao Tzu > Quotes > Quotable Quotes," Goodreads.com, http:// www.goodreads.com/quotes/46410-a-leader-is-best-when-people-barely-know-he- exists, accessed January 7, 2016.

30 Kellerman, *The End of Leadership*, Kindle edition, introduction.

31 Karp and Helgø, "Leadership as Identity Construction," 884.

32 I am an avid reader who values seminars and books. Eliminating or naysaying these tools is not my intent. Using them within the larger context of identity is.

33 "When members of the Stanford Graduate School of Business Advisory Council were asked to recommend the most important capability for leaders to develop, they answered 'self-awareness.'" Karp and Helgø, "Leadership as Identity Construction," 888, citing B. George and P. Sims, *True North: Discover Your Authentic Leadership* (San Francisco: Jossey-Bass, 2007).

34 Ibid., 888.

35 Karp and Helgø, "Leadership as Identity Construction," 888.

36 Karp and Helgø, "Leadership as Identity Construction," 892.

37 Indiana High School Athletic Association, *Captain's Handbook*, http:// www.ihsaa.org/portals/0/ihsaa/documents/membership/captains%20handbook.pdf, accessed December10, 2015; emphasis added.

38 Karp and Helgø, "Leadership as Identity Construction," 884.

39 Mr. Drucker was quoted in Jim Clemmer's book,